BUSINESS MADE EASY

ABIMBOLA BABATUNDE

DEDICATION

This book is dedicated to God Almighty my creator, Lord Jesus my savior and Redeemer; The Holy Spirit, my comforter and foundation of my knowledge and to the memories of my late mother Mrs Mosekola Abimbola.

AKNOWLEDGEMENT

All good and perfect gifts come from God the master designer of all fountains of knowledge to him I owe all glory. I am officially humbled by the supports I have received towards the success of this thesis.

Many thanks to my immediate family, my siblings, my dad: Elder Gabriel Abimbola, my wife Olawunmi Abimbola and my sons Alexander Oluwadarasimi Abimbola and Bright Oluwanifemi Abimbola for their encouragement and understanding in the course of writing this book.

Not forgetting my spiritual family Emmanuel Gospel Youth fellowship and all those who contributed to my moral, spiritual, educational and professional training.

I appreciate my benefactors, those who fear God, those who crave for success, those who are devoted to just course and the common good of mankind.

TABLE OF CONTENT

INTRODUCTION

The desire and urge to get rich is prevalent in our contemporary society. The fact remains that the true there is a thin line between success and failure. It is bridged by the will of man.

To attain success the ability and the will power to succeed can be developed through trying to be independent and taking the pain to generate self-made income and self-made wealth.

This can only be achieved through venturing into a business. However, Taking great steps like doing a business may appear risky and uncertain, but if well planned in line with strong desire and strategy, it is really worthwhile.

This book focuses on guiding us through business tips that can make us great entrepreneurs and serve as an exposition towards what it takes to start and succeed in a business.

CHAPTER ONE

LEVEL OF EARNINGS?

To be employed is good, its an activity which brings expectation on a monthly basis, at least basic needs an be met.

However, the fact remains that human wants is on satiable. Money can't fight inflation because what you can get for for certain amount now can go for the same price in five year from now. Our needs on the otherhand keeps growing and increasing.

If as a single you earn #50,000 now and all your needs are just #30,000 you may look confortable, but when you become married and you are on the same salary, life may not be comfortable.

The issue of need is an ever growing and cannot come to an end till death. Therefore, it is advisable one builds a system to fight ones need in the nearest.

According to Kiyosaki " From 1960 to 2000 the value of dollar as declined steadily"

"When you take a look at this 40-years run on the dollar, the dollar is designed economically to loose money every single year. So, why would you save somtheing that loses money every year?

And what does this mean for you or for somebody on the retirement plans, if the value of the dollar goes down and your cost of living keeps going up after you retire?

This suffice to say that Kiyosaki does not support savings as a mean of combating inflation rather for one to do a business that gives and edge again future needs.

Robert Kiyosaki in his cash flow quadrant gave this illustration.

He identified 4 level of earnings

1. The employed: He/shw who is under an employemt of another and get salary/wages as a reward for his/her Labour and time. The employed as long as he or she is in service is a slave of the master and meant to carry out instructions as given by the boss.
2. The Self employed: He/she can be considered as independent and not timc bound to the employer. One of the problem encountered in this category lack of enough capital to meet up business.
3. The business system owners: They enjoy leverage and make people work for them they have time to strategise and plan to make their business big. Time is sufficient to relax and plan bigger businesses. The people in this category put the burden of their business on other and pay them for taken such burden.
4. The Investors: Its and advance stage of being a business system owner. People in this category send their money on errand. Their money work for them and its being used to generate money.

However from the aforementioned you can figure out the category one wish to find yourself. Although, there are many criticism posited against Kiyosaki, popular among them was that of Evan Vanderbuilt where he said Multi Level Marketing is not the business of the 21st Century. According to him, "In realty, the MLM-dominated direct selling industry in the U.S. has not proven to be an increasingly important alternative to traditional store retailing in the 21st century. Corporate America has outperformed MLM. MLM companies haven't seen significant growth in the U.S. market in decades" I would not like us to be much bothered about their argument, but should be focused on how we can be susccessful business owners whether we are engaged in Multi-Level marketing, Direct selling, retailing, wholesaling , service rendering e.tc.

Having discussed the level of earnings, one may say that before starting the big business one needs to start small, This book as promised, will help us to understand the level of businesses that can be ventured into and one can take things a step at a time.

CHAPTER TWO

WHAT IS BUSINESS?

Tips from Wikipedia makes us to understand that "A business, also known as an enterprise or a firm, is an organization involved in the trade of goods, services, or both to consumers.[1] Businesses are prevalent in capitalist economies, where most of them are privately owned and provide goods and services to customers in exchange for other goods, services, or money. Businesses may also be not-for-profit or state-owned. A business owned by multiple individuals may be referred to as a company.

Typical samples of the different types of business organisation are explained below:

Sole traders: Simply put, a One man Business. Examples are like small corner stores and newsagents. If you call out a plumber or electrician they have a good chance of being a sole trader. Although they may also be part of a franchise arrangement or a partnership.

Partnership : Formation of this is company is by two or more people who come together to pool resources together inorder to achieve comman good..

Private companies - are typically small family businesses that want to keep the control of the business within the family.

Public companies - are the well known national and international companies like Nestle, NBC e.t.c

Franchises - are commonly found in Quick Service Restaurants such as Mr Biggs. McDonald's as well as in other food outlets.

Limited liability - is a form of business protection for company shareholders and some limited partners. For these individuals the maximum sum they can lose from a business venture, into which they have contributed going bust, is the sum of money that they have invested in the company - this is the limit of their liability.

Cooperative-Often referred to as a "co-op", a cooperative is a limited liability business that can organize for-profit or not-for-profit. A cooperative differs from a corporation in that it has member, not shareholders, and they share decision-making authority. Cooperatives are typically classified as either consumer cooperatives or worker cooperatives. Cooperatives are fundamental to the ideology of economic democracy.

There is an adage by the Yorubas an ethnic group in Nigeria a west African country that says "ise omo alase je, owo omo alase la" this local aphorism simple implies that when you have a paid job, it's usually done to put food on one's table but trade or business is that which can only make one to be wealthy.

This aphorism does not suffice to say that there are people who are successful working for an organization, may be few who are lucky to work for one of the multinationals or big corporations, yes they are.

But it can be seen clearly that that no matter the number of years spent by this people they are not as wealthy as the owner of business.

The table below will give us an idea.

S/N	STAFF	NOS	SALARY MONTHLY	TOTAL MONTHLY	TOTAL PER ANNUM
1	Directors	6	2,000,000	12,000,000	144,000,000
2	GM-AGMS	10	1,500,000	15,000,000	180,000,000
3	Senior Managers	15	1,200,000	18,000,000	216,000,000
4	Managers	25	800,000	20,000,000	240,000,000
5	Senior Staff	100	400,000	40,000,000	480,000,000
6	Junior	200	150,000	30,000,000	360,000,000
7	Contracts	100	70,000	7,000,000	84,000,000
8	Casuals	100	40,000	4,000,000	48,000,000
	Total	556	6,160,000	146,000,000	1,752,000,000

This shows clearly that no worker can ever earn as much as the owner of business because if a man agrees to pay 2million per month how much is the man himself making for himself.

We may say that this table is over exaggerated, but we can draw our table either on paper or in our mind, the fact remains that the employer will always earn more.

Some of the educational qualification and ideas of the employed professionals are used to rake money into another man's pocket. A careful look at the forbes and some other body rating wealthy people locally in the world, we would see clearly that very good percentage if not all is made up of people in one line of business or the other ranging from , IT, Telecoms, trading, real estate, oil and gas, banking, stocks, merchandizing etc. Example of such men are: Our own Aliko Dangote, Mike Adenuga, Otedola, Jim Ovia, Oba Otudeko, Warren Buffet, Zuckerberg, Bill gate to mention but a few. I have not seen anyone on the list that is in paid employment.

I cannot deny the fact that there are challenges in doing a business especially like a country like Nigeria. We shall quickly examine some known challenges related to doing business in Nigeria.

CHAPTER THREE

WHY I CAN'T DO BUSINESS?

The fact cannot be denied that many people face challenges in their bid of thinking of doing business.

These challenges are real and true and should not be shy aware from. The Challenges of Doing Business in Nigeria are as follows:

1. Lack of Infrastructure

The first business challenge you will face when doing business in Nigeria is infrastructural challenge. Nigeria lacks the basic infrastructure and logistics to support entrepreneurship. If you are going to run a successful business in Nigeria; then you must have the financial muscle to provide your own infrastructure.

Take for instance you want to start a manufacturing firm in Nigeria; you will need to build your own factory, provide your own water supply and other amenities that smoothens business operations.

This single factor lengthens the time frame from initial planning to full business operations when compared to developed countries that have the basic infrastructure in place. Infrastructural challenge will directly or indirectly increase your startup overhead cost so you have to properly factor in this challenge in your business plan.

2. Poor Power Supply

Poor power supply is the next challenge militating against the successful growth of small business startups in Nigeria. Successful companies operating in Nigeria has found a way to deal with the challenge of power supply by providing their own power.

For instance, Aliko Dangote; the founder of Dangote Group has developed the strategy of situating a mini power plant right next to his factories as an alternative to the erratic power supply in the company. So if you are successfully going to operate in Nigeria; then you must map out a plan to curtail the harsh effect of poor power supply.

3. Inadequate Security

Security is the next challenge you must deal with especially if you are a foreigner wanting to invest in building a business in Nigeria. But I think it's worthwhile I add that there has been a massive step up by the government with respect to security and based on this; I can confidently say that I am impressed with the way the government is handling the security of the state. However, I don't think the security challenge is going away anytime soon; so you have to be prepared to deal with it.

4. Inconsistent Government Policies

Government inconsistency is really a challenge you will have to tackle if you must succeed in Nigeria as an entrepreneur. Governance is something entrepreneurs have no control over; all entrepreneurs can do is try to influence government's policy with respect to enacting favorable business laws. But you must have political clout and massive resources to be able to influence government laws.

Now you may not have the political clout or financial muscle to influence government's policy so the best strategy to combating the ever changing policy of the government is to keep a keen eye on government laws and swiftly adjust your business to align with the policies.

5. Transportation Challenges

The next challenge of doing business in Nigeria is the poor transportation standard. As expected; the dependable source of raw materials you need may not be situated close to your target market. So you will have to decide if to locate your business close to the raw materials or close to your market. Either way; transportation of either raw materials or finished goods will be involved and this will pose a great challenge if you intend operating in Nigeria.

Poor transportation standard and road network is a factor militating against industrialization in Nigeria but I believe this challenge is being tackled by the government through the upgrading of roads and construction of railway lines.

6. Inability to access funds

Of all the business challenges involved with starting a small business in Nigeria; this one interest entrepreneurs the most. Inability to access funds and banks unwillingness to support entrepreneurship and small business is the major barrier to massive entrepreneurship growth in Nigeria.

However, this challenge can be surmounted if you are a die hard, creative entrepreneur. Hard core entrepreneurs are not held back by the lack of support from banks; they are not discouraged by the unavailability of startup capital. Rather than lament over the predicament, they look for creative ways to finance their business plans and ideas.

So if you are in this category of entrepreneurs; then I want to believe that your plans of doing business in Nigeria will not be thwarted or held back by the challenge of capital. I have notice that contrary to what people think. Capital is not the greatest challenge of starting a business; the greatest challenge is getting a very good business idea.

7. Lack of Governmental Support

The last but not the least challenge of doing business in Nigeria is government's insensitivity to the plight of entrepreneurs and small business owners. And the result of these insensitivity surfaces in the form of double taxation, corruption, unnecessary levies and duties, bureaucratic bottlenecks at various government agencies like CAC, NAFDAC, etc; and high cost of obtaining business licenses.

But Nigeria operates as a free economy; which favors capitalists, so I don't think you will be discouraged by this challenge. A good strategy to balance the excesses of the government is to have a strong business team that will strategically position your business to withstand the ever increasing demand of the government

Aside from the aforementioned, the following questions may may also arise that how does one survive in a business that one does not know about and how do one raise capital to start a business.

This issue is a long aged issue in a startup business and I will not shy aware to address it in the cause of this chapter.

An understanding of Terry Powell's "Three steps to eliminating the barriers to becoming self-sufficient" will guide us a bit in overcoming the fear of experience and capital.

While 75 percent of people are interested in becoming self-sufficient, only 5 percent are ready, willing and able to act on their dream. Of all the obstacles facing individuals, fear is the most paralyzing. When exploring all their options to become self-sufficient, weighing risks and rewards, the variables involved are often punctuated by fear. While being afraid can promote caution when venturing into something new, it can also be paralyzing and may prevent people from chasing success.

Pay attention to your gut feelings and don't ignore your concerns, but put fear in its place. What if you were to find out that your fear is based on False Evidence Appearing Real, would that change your perspective? Each year there will be obstacles that you perceive as barriers to venturing into something new, like changing your career path and exploring whether entrepreneurship or business ownership is right for you. It will never seem like the right time, so we encourage you not to make any decisions in haste, rather educate yourself about the vehicles or options available that will lead you to your dream of self-sufficiency. Start by considering these three strategies to finally pursue your dreams:

Start with why.

What is your "why"? Asking "why," in regards to a new career path, will set a proper foundation for effectively exploring the best possibilities and evaluating options to realize your dreams of self-sufficiency. Identifying your primary aim in life will be the driving force. It will be the why behind the what. Identify your strengths and weaknesses as some of these could be transferable skills. Next think about your short and long term goals in terms of ILWE – Income, Lifestyle, Wealth and Equity. What kind of income would you like to generate, what kind of lifestyle would you like to live, what kind of wealth and equity would you like to build and acquire? This will lay the groundwork on which you can build the next version of you.

Keep an open mind and embrace the unknown.

Did you know, the most successful business owners frequently aren't experts within the field in which they own a business? They have figured out that doing what you know, love and enjoy does not guarantee success. Further they also have figured out that you don't necessarily need to be in love with a product or service to capitalize on it. They are in the business of business. They use the business as a vehicle to attain their why, their income, lifestyle, wealth and equity goals. Being afraid of the unknown could potentially stifle future success and lead you down the wrong path.

Seek a safe haven.

The first step toward success is having a solid foundation. Evaluate potential opportunities and options against that to better irrational and limiting fears. Find a trusted confidant to keep you grounded and provide you with objective advice and support. As we've all been told repeatedly, there is no such thing as a stupid question. Don't allow yourself to miss out on important opportunities and information by not asking. But be aware, there are dream catchers and dream stealers. Be sure to align yourself with someone who will support your dreams and ask questions, not someone who knowingly or unknowingly will lead you down a path based on their own fears. Someone like an alternative coach will be able to give insight on unexpected complications and help you to see your possibilities.

With any new life adventure, there will be obstacles. Becoming self-sufficient and exploring whether owning your own business is right for you means it's up to you to find the motivation and support to overcome said obstacles and persevere through anything that comes your way. Gain clarity about what you want while keeping an open mind in regard to your options. Build a support system and do not succumb to fear rooted in false evidence appearing real. This year you could be among the five percent of people who are pursuing their dream of self-sufficiency.

One fact remains that experience cannot be totally over ruled when starting business, for example people for anyone who wants to go into a distributive trade business, it is required that such person has an experience in sales. But it does not necessarily mean that one cannot start without having experience what Powell suggests is that a short training or seeking advice from an expert can also help because No matter how hard you study and try, you will never know it all and that's why you need business coaches, advisors or mentors. They will help you avoid some deadly mistakes that most startups make in their early stage. Now that my fears are all eliminated then do I start my business?

CHAPTER FOUR

HOW TO START A BUSINESS

The basic facts and reality associated with doing a business are itemized and analysed below.

1. Any sane person can do business:

Business can be done not necessarily with a formal education, though the fact cannot be denied that formal education can help a great deal in business but the most important thing is how sane the person is. Any person in his /her right frame of mind can do and succeed in a business.

2. You do not need a large capital to begin:

This is another big misconception about doing a business; people believe that one need huge amount of money to start. The first thing one need is the will **power and gut** to begin. Also the **idea** of what one needs to do is also crucial.

If these are not put in place, it is possible one have money and not know what to do with it and when one does not have a clear direction of what to do in mind he/she can venture into the business and lose all the money.

3. Business is grown:

Business is like a building which begins from foundation. No business gets to peak without its early beginning. They always start from the scratch.

Take a study of any multinational company that comes to your mind and you will understand they all have their humble beginning.

4. Business can be learnt.

It is possible someone may be born a business guru, but if you are not born as one, you can strive to grow into one. The thing to do is to follow basic principle of business and see it shoots to ones desired level.

The following are the benefits of having a business know how.

1. The possibility of making money through the training process: Having a paid job before starting your own business may bring an avenue to have the required fund to startup instead of the pain and challenge most people face to begin.
2. Learning about the business can bring the needed connections. When you learn about a business, it may enable you to know where you can get raw material, those to buy from and also help to know where and those to sell to.
3. Learning about a trade or business enables you to have a technical know-how and be able to run professionally and profitably.

How to Start a Business

1. Make the decision to start your own business

No one wakes up and opens a business; you must first make up your mind and prepare yourself for the challenges of the business world. Now why do u want to become an entrepreneur? How do you know if starting a business is for you? You can begin by checking your present financial status. Most people come to me asking me how to become a millionaire fast; but i laugh and tell them i don't know. Starting a business to become a millionaire is not a good enough reason to do it.

Are you contented with where you are now? Are you in control of your financial future? Are you tired of your job and want to quit? Do you have brilliant small business ideas within you? These questions will help you decide if to start a business or not. But whatever your reason for starting a business; make sure that it is strong enough to propel you through the several business challenges you will encounter.

2. Develop your mindset

The next step to starting a small business is to develop your mindset and toughen your skin against competition and challenges of building a business. To succeed in business, you need to possess the mindset of the likes of Bill Gates, Donald Trump, Steve Jobs, Henry Ford, etc.

3. Sharpen your business skills

"*Skill*" and "*competence*" is what separate the successful entrepreneurs from the mediocre. Without having the right business skills, forget about becoming an entrepreneur. Example of business skills you need include selling skill, accounting skill, leadership skill, negotiation skill, etc.

4. Create a business idea or find a business opportunity

The idea is the foundation on which any business is built. It could be a service or a product idea but it needs to be solid and should solve a problem. The bottom line of your idea should be to solve a certain problem.

5. Conduct feasibility study

The world is filled with brilliant million dollar ideas; but the world lack brilliant entrepreneurs. Most business die without getting off the drawing board; they never cross the idea development stage. Now how do you differentiate a winning small business idea from a dead one? How much does it cost to start a business? How do you decide if a business opportunity is worth pursuing or not? How much money do you need to start a business? Only a feasibility report holds the answer to all these questions.

6. Write a business plan

Most entrepreneurs don't know how to write a business plan; so they launch their businesses without a plan. You can keep yourself ahead of others by writing a business plan for your idea. But you shouldn't allow the process of making a business plan result to analysis paralysis and hinder your launch. Remember that in business and investing, timing is everything.

7. Incorporate your business

Most businesses operate as sole proprietorships, general partnership and limited partnerships. But if you are really serious about building a solid business that can grow without you, then you must incorporate your business. The resources below will be of tremendous help to you.

8. Start the business

If you diligently follow all steps then you are set to launch your business. At this stage, you can choose to start a home based business and work from home or open a business within a corporate district.

9. Build a business team

Business is a team sport, so also is investing. One untold reason why most businesses stay small and fail after five years is because they are competing against well-organized businesses and strong management teams. If you plan to build a big business, then you need your own business team.

12. Grow your business

Growing a business requires discipline and a whole lot of professionalism. A business that is not well managed and its fund is beings misappropriated will dry up.

CHAPTER FIVE

BUSINESS SUGGESTIONS & RECOMMENDATIONS

25 Medium scale business ideas and opportunities in Nigeria.

The writer of these business tips called it small scale business, but I will refer to them as large or medium scale because some of them are capital intensive and are beyond what a common Nigerian can afford to venture into.
But if you have the financial strength to engage in them you will not have a regret doing so.

1. Livestock Farming

Livestock farming is a booming business in Nigeria and the trend is not dying anytime soon. With 150+million mouths to feed daily, there will always be demand for livestock products. However, lack of technical know-how and the use of crude equipment are the major factors hampering the growth of this industry. If you can come in with adequate knowledge and the patience to nurture this business, you will reap immensely. Now you can choose to either venture into livestock breeding of animals or better still, you can stick to livestock feed production or equipment retailing.

A. Poultry farming – Egg production, meat production, hatchery or day-old-chicks production, etc.
B. Cattle Farming – Diary (*milk*) production, beef, etc.
C. Goat Farming
D. Sheep
E. Fish Farming
F. Piggery
G. Grasscutter Farming
H. Snail Farming

2. Agro-products exportation

Nigeria is blessed with a lot of food and natural resources; and most of these natural resources are raw materials needed for the production of some finished products. Every day, tons of raw materials and food products leave the shores of Nigeria to countries such as India, Vietnam, China, USA, UK, Brazil, etc; yet, the demand is never met. You can become an exporter by simply registering with the Nigerian Export Promotion Council and decide on the specific product you wish to export. Examples of products highly in demand are *Chili pepper, Kola nuts, Bitter Kola, Cassava flakes (Garri), Cocoa, Groundnut, Yam flour, Cashew nuts,* etc.

3. Mining

Nigeria is blessed with a lot of mineral resources like Limestone, Coal, Iron ore, Bitumen, etc. Aside this, the mining industry in Nigeria is set to take off because the federal government in June

2013 implemented a policy to drive forward the mining industry by declaring the importation of mining equipment duty free. The government is also going after many dormant investors who were granted mining licenses but are not utilizing it. This act I believe, will spur the growth in the mining sector. If you have the financial capacity and a team, you can position yourself in this sector.

4. Setting up a private mini refinery

There are lots of business opportunities in the oil and gas sector. Building a private refinery and refining crude oil is another business you should look into because there is a lot of potential in it. In January 2012, the federal government announced the partial removal of subsidy and with a long term plan to totally remove fuel subsidy. What this means in essence is that petroleum product importers will now sell as they buy; thus bringing in competition and it is a known fact that 80% of petroleum products consumed in Nigeria are imported. Now with the total removal of fuel subsidy, investors will now have the opportunity to set up their own refinery and produce fuel. Are you among those that think the total fuel subsidy removal is a pipe dream? Then think again because in May 2013, Aliko Dangote raised $4billion for the setting up of a refinery; which will be sited in Ondo state. Enough said.

5. Inland waterway Transport

There are lots of opportunities in the transport industry and inland waterway is one of them. Nigeria has a broad network of inland waterways comprising rivers, creeks, lakes and seas; yet, transportation still remains a challenge because investors are yet to tap into water transportation. A lot of countries such as Italy, Thailand, etc have effectively been utilizing their waterways as a means of transport; thus reducing the traffic congestion on the road. All you need to do is to incorporate a company, obtain license from the state and federal government, import or purchase some locally fabricated boats; and you are in business.

6. Establishing a Television and Radio Station

Now it is a known fact that the mass media industry is saturated in Nigeria. However, this is only true for some cities in Nigeria such as Lagos and Abuja. I have travel through several parts of the countries and discovered that most states have no private TV station, and only rely on the government own TV stations; which are very incompetent, uncreative and unreliable. I see an opportunity for entrepreneurs and investor with interest and competence in broadcasting or mass media. You can either choose to setup a radio station or TV Station.

7. Setting up a security company
There is a huge demand for excellent security services in Nigeria. As the government battle to improve the security situation in the country, individuals and corporate entities are now becoming aware of the fact that security is not the responsibility of the government alone; it is a collective responsibility. Hence, the current increase in demand for security guards, bodyguards, executive protection professionals and security gadgets or devices. As an entrepreneur or investor, you can setup a security guard recruitment or training company, or you can setup a bodyguard agency. Also, you can import and retail security products and safety devices.

8. Sewing of specialized uniforms
There are over 500 schools (both Crèche, primary and secondary) in Lagos state alone; and each of these schools have a specific uniform or attire for their students. Okay, let's look beyond educational institutions. Do you know that other individuals and corporate organizations are in need of uniforms for their security personnel, staff, etc? There are also a lot or military (Army, Air Force, Navy), paramilitary (Civil Defense Corps, Police Force) and non-paramilitary (Road Safety, Traffic Warden, Kick against Indiscipline, Vigilante groups, etc) organizations in Nigeria that make use of uniforms. You can position yourself as a uniform supplier and make money from it.

9. Construction company
Nigeria is still a developing country especially in the area of infrastructure but this is set to change in the nearest future. Massive constructions are currently on-going in Nigeria ranging from bridges, roads, towers and skyscrapers, etc. If you run a construction company oversee, or you have the financial capacity to

assemble the needed team and machinery for a construction company; then this is a business you should invest in.

10. Real Estate development

I have met a lot of individuals with money piling up in the bank, but they don't seem to know what to do with that money. Yet, on every business trip I make, I hear stories of people facing accommodation problems; not because they can't afford it but because there is none within their choice of location. Also, I hear woeful stories from students in various universities and other high institutions who live under harsh conditions; not because they want to or can't afford a comfortable place to live; but because they is no conducive apartment in close proximity to the institutions.

I also know the stress, effort and resources it took me before I got an office space both within and outside Lagos. What these facts or complaints are pointing to is that there is a massive need for buildings, both residential and commercial. It is a known fact that shelter is one of the basic needs of man. Now for those who wouldn't want to go through the ups and downs of running a business, you can choose to invest in development of hotels, school hostels for students, shopping malls, residential apartments, events and conference halls, etc.

11. Set up a writing company

If you are current with trend, you would have observed that most jobs in the United States are now being outsourced to countries like Philippines, India, China, etc. And as things stand now, a trickle of such outsourcing jobs are coming to Nigeria and one of such jobs is Article Writing or Ghostwriting. Do you have passion and skill for writing? If yes, then you can either choose to write from home as a self employed freelance writer or you can setup a company, employ competent writers and source for job online. This business is easy to get into and it is very profitable.

12. Call center agency

Have you called the customer care service of a telecom network before? Or have you tried sending a message or complaint to a corporate organization before? Do you know that those who take your calls, complaints and respond accordingly are not employees of the companies you patronize; neither do they operate in the premises of the company. If you are hearing this for the first time, then welcome to the world of "Call center outsourcing." You can setup a call center agency and work for big companies on a contract basis. One sweet fact about this business is that you can start it from home and it doesn't require much startup capital unless you want to scale up by employing more helping hands.

13. Recruitment Agency

The labour market is becoming tougher and there are over five million unemployed youths in Nigeria. Another hard fact is that companies are no longer employing full time in-house staff; they are now using the services of recruitment agencies to employ people based on contract basis. This strategy is aimed at reducing the cost of doing business by avoiding the cost of conducting a recruitment exercise and also avoiding employee claims and benefits. This is the sole reason why banks and other companies are sacking their workers on daily basis. So rather than fight the trend, why not profit from it by setting up a recruitment agency and connect jobseekers to their dream jobs. You can also be a corporate executive headhunter and make money poaching competent staff from one company to another.

14. Importation of wears

Clothing is another basic need of man. Regardless of the economy, people must wear clothes and this includes shoes, bags, underwear, perfumes, etc. Now there is a fast growing trend now and that is "Used clothes" or "Recycled clothes." Since the economy is getting tougher and there's need to be clothed, the masses have resolved to buying used clothes rather than new ones. Still yet, there is a market for new clothes; for men, women, and kids. You can source your materials from China, Hong Kong, Italy, France, Dubai, India, etc.

15. Haulage and logistics

Haulage and logistics is another booming business in Nigeria because regardless of the weather, people must haul their goods from one location to another. In fact, haulage or trucking business is one of the most profitable businesses so far; though it is management intensive. However, you can start with just a truck and see how it goes. You can choose to focus on hauling containers for clients from the seaports to their various destinations or better still, you can choose to haul products of specific companies such as breweries, production companies, etc. You can also haul perishable goods from farms and villages to the marketplace or you can haul specialty products such as frozen foods, petroleum products, gas, etc. Now there is also an opportunity for those who want to venture into haulage business but do not want to be bugged down by management requirements. All you need to do is to buy a truck and contract it to a Haulage and logistics company; which will in turn pay you a specified amount weekly or monthly based on agreement.

16. Outsourced bus service

This is another form of haulage business, but this time you will be lifting humans. This is a business that requires providing transportation services to organizations that cannot afford to buy a vehicle in-house. Your clients in this case can be schools, religious organizations, NGOs, etc. Now just imagine providing a bus and a driver, to be shared by three or more schools that can't afford to own their own private bus; and you will catch the vision of this business.

17. e-Services

Nigeria is catching on with the rest of the world with respect to technology. If you are technologically inclined, you can setup shop in Nigeria and start offering e-services to clients. Example of such e-services include Web designing and development, App development, Digital marketing services, Search Engine Optimization services, Banner design services, Bulk SMS services, Online registration of exams such as JAMB, WAEC, professional courses, etc

18. Daycare centre

The demand for quality childcare service is increasing daily. Parents are now working harder just to generate enough income to keep the family going, thus leaving them with less time for the children. Now to be honest with you, there are a lot of daycare centers existing but only a few are providing exceptional services; and parents that cherish their kids are never comfortable leaving their kids in a child care centre whose environment is dirty. If you can come in with exceptional service and creativity, you will make money from this business. Another thing you must know is that you can start this Business from home.

19. Training centers

Every year, millions of people sit for examinations and tests in Nigeria and most of these people usually need some kind of trainings or tutorials. You can position yourself as a provider of such training and make money off this niche. Examples of trainings you can offer include skill vocational acquisition training, corporate management skill training, etc. You can also conduct tutorial for individuals writing professional exams like ICAN, WAEC, JAMB, A. LEVEL, etc.

20. Waste Management

Waste management is another business with a future potential because Nigerians are yet to imbibe the habit of proper waste disposal. However, states like Lagos have been doing a lot to encourage proper waste disposal and management. Now there are several businesses you can start within the waste management niche and these include waste recycling, waste disposal, junk hauling, organic fertilizer production, etc.

21. Food processing

Another profitable industry to consider is the food processing industry. The concept of this industry is simply to take raw food material and turn them into finished products. In fact, there are a lot of businesses you can do in this niche and examples of such businesses include Tomato puree production, Garri Processing, oil palm processing, groundnut processing, Fruit juice production, Rice milling, etc.

22. Alternative Power Installation

As the world goes green, and Nigeria battles her power supply challenges; there is an already established opening in Nigeria's power sector. Even though the government has taken steps to deregulate the power sector by granting licenses for Independent

Power Plants, granting a free import duty for the importation of power generation equipment and commissioning several power projects, this will never hamper the growing demand for alternative power generators such as solar panels, wind mills, Inverters, etc. You can either make money by importing and retailing these materials or you can choose to focus on installations.

23. Plantation Farming
Do you have a fertile vacant land and you know that you won't be developing any structure on it in the nearest future? Then why not start a livestock farming, crop cultivation or plantation farming. There are a lot of cash crops you can plant, nurture and forget; and they will keep providing you with steady returns annually. Examples of crops you can start a plantation around are Orange, Plantain, Kola nut, Oil palm, Cocoa, Cassava, Yam, etc.

24. Manufacturing
You can also venture into small scale manufacturing of products that are in daily need. You don't need to build a factory or industrial plant; you can start on a small scale from your room or a rented store or apartment. Products you can start manufacturing include Toothpick, Tissue paper, Serviette, chalk production, candle, Match sticks, nylons and polythene bags, cartons, paper bags, etc.

25. Bottled water production
I get calls from individuals almost on daily basis who are interested in setting up a "sachet water" (Pure water) production plant. Now let me tell you the honest truth, the sachet water or pure water business is saturated and the business may die off very soon. Why did I say this? Well, I got information from a reliable source that there is a long term plan to ban the production of sachet or nylon water; so as to stem environmental degradation and checkmate blocked drainages. So once this bill is passed into law, the sachet water production industry is toast. The only solution I foresee that can keep this business afloat is the establishment of a nylon recycling plant. However, to avoid being a victim of this yet-to-be proposed policy, it is advisable you venture into bottled water products and establish yourself as a brand.

Source: My top business ideas

However, for the purpose of those who have very low capital and may not be able to venture in to the aforementioned businesses.

Below are the small scale businesses carely selected and recommended for you.

1. Catering services (Indoor and Outdoor)
2. Mobile food vendoring
3. Computer training centre
4. Cement sales and distribution
5. Cyber café
6. Froozen foods sales
7. Rental services
8. Sales of Used cars
9. Blogging
10. Freelancing
11. Cooking gas sales
12. Transportation
13. Online marketing
14. Bulk SMS service
15. Photography and videography
16. Printing and book production
17. Make up artiste
18. Solar energy installation & Equipement sales
19. Antique Furniture sales
20. Disc Jockey (DJ)
21. Laundry Service
22. Fashion Stylist
23. Modelling and Event Ushering
24. House Painting
25. Funeral arrangement company
26. Car rentals
27. Day care centre/crèche
28. Sport viewing centre
29. Sport betting agency
30. Travelling agency
31. Building block production

32. Recharge card sales
33. Cleaning service
34. Hairdressing Salon
35. Pedicure and manicure service
36. Selling fruits
37. Selling Honey
38. Car wash and detailing service
39. Video Game centre
40. Nanny agency
41. Ice block production
42. Security gadget sales & installation
43. Cable Tv installation
44. Affiliate marketing
45. Ice cream & cake production
46. Mobile phone sales & accessories
47. Computer repair & accessories sales
48. Pure & bottled water production
49. Live stock farming
50. Poultry farming
51. Social media marketing
52. Mini-Importation
53. Recruitment Agency
54. Small scale manucfacturing
55. Waste management service
56. Art gallery
57. Jewelry making
58. Magazine publication
59. Monogramming & branding service
60. Private library service
61. Restaurant
62. Alternative power supply
63. Marketing
64. Virtual assistant
65. Pest Control
66. Art Broker
67. Resume writing
68. SEQ Consultant
69. Gift Basket
70. Faciclities management

CHAPTER SIX

FINANCING YOUR BUSINESS

One of the most critical challenges entrepreneurs face is raising funds and unfortunately, raising capital is the primary task of an entrepreneur because without it; even the best of ideas will not survive.

I want to proffer two basic means of financing a business which I call the dependent and independent mean.

Dependent:

1. Borrowing from friends and relatives: One can approach people who are related to you or those you have close contact with for financial help.

However, to really get them to assist you, you may have to discuss the viability of your business with them. If the business is viable and they can reason with you on how profitable it can be, the job is half done and they are likely going to assist.

2. Partnering:

3. Loans: Loan is another mean of generating fund to finance a business. It's usually given on an agreed interest rate and most times collateral and a guarantor may be required. Collateral demanded are mostly gold, cars and landed properties with C of O. (Certificate of Occupancy).

   Loan can be accessed from most Microfinance bank, mortgage and finances and some commercial banks all over the country.

Independent:

1. Personal savings: Saving; is another mean of financing a business. Like the saying goes "little drop of water makes a mighty ocean" saving money which you may not necessarily need at a point can generate into lump sum that can be used to do a business. In my next book, I will be expatiating on this aspect on likely ways to safe for the long term.

2. Outsource your skill: It can help to make a side income while growing your business. Our skill can be means of making money to boost our business. Anyone with a business mindset can make money from certain skills he or she has and use such money to boost business.

3. Get paid to or through network: There are many multi-level marketing programme that one can participate in to raise money from which one can fund his/her business thereafter. I advise one should be careful because some of this programmes are scam, but the fact remain that good ones abounds.

CHAPTER SEVEN

TIPS TO INVESTING

Having discussed about business, another mean of accumulation wealth is investment. Investment is a giant step business owner can take. It is not peculiar to successful business system owner alone, but also individuals with accumulated money which may be from business or well-paid job piling up at a corner of the room or bank.

My point is that one of the many ways of accumulating wealth over the time is investment.

Depending on the amount of money you have to play with investment is not peculiar to trading stocks only, but also some other profitable ventures which are capable of yielding increase over the long term.

Investing is the act of committing money or capital to an endeavor with the expectation of obtaining an additional income or profit. In another word, it simply means putting your money to work for you.

According to investopedia, there are many different ways you can go about making an investment. This includes putting money into stocks, bonds, mutual funds, or real estate (among many other things), or starting your own business. Sometimes people refer to these options as "investment vehicles," which is just another way of saying "a way to invest." Each of these vehicles has positives and negatives. The point is that it doesn't matter which method you choose for investing your money, the goal is always to put your money to work so it earns you an additional profit. Even though this is a simple idea, it's the most important concept for you to understand.

It should be noted that gambling or betting should not be termed as investing, because this is highly risky and it is full of uncertainty as it is a game of luck. If one dabble into such activity he/she is not certain of getting returns.

1. Stocks:
Stock is simply the capital raised by a company or corporation through the issue and subscription of shares. The Following are facts that we ought to know about stocks.

(A) Stocks give us ownership

When you buy a share of stock, you are taking a share of ownership in a company. Collectively, the company is owned by all the shareholders, and each share represents a claim on assets and earnings.

(B) There are many different kinds of stocks.

The most common ways to divide the market are by company size (measured by market capitalization), sector, and types of growth patterns. Investors may talk about large-cap vs. small-cap stocks, energy vs. technology stocks, or growth vs. value stocks, for example.

(C.) Stock prices track earnings.

Over the short term, the behavior of the market is based on enthusiasm, fear, rumors and news. Over the long term, though, it is mainly company earnings that determine whether a stock's price will go up, down or sideways.

(D) Stocks are your best shot for getting a return over and above the pace of inflation.

Since the end of World War II, through many ups and downs, the average large stock has returned close to 10% a year -- well ahead of inflation, and the return of bonds, real estate and other savings vehicles. As a result, stocks are the best way to save money for long-term goals like retirement.

(E) Individual stocks are not the market.

A good stock may go up even when the market is going down, while a bad can go down even when the market is booming.

(F) A great track record does not guarantee strong performance in the future.

Stock prices are based on projections of future earnings. A strong track record bodes well, but even the best companies can slip.

(G) You can't tell how expensive a stock is by looking only at its price.

Because a stock's value depends on earnings, a # 1.00 stock can be cheap if the company's earnings prospects are high enough, while a #2.00 stock can be expensive if earnings potential is dim.

(H) Investors compare stock prices to other factors to assess value.

To get a sense of whether a stock is over- or undervalued, investors compare its price to revenue, earnings, cash flow, and other fundamental criteria. Comparing a company's performance expectations to those of its industry is also common -- firms operating in slow-growth industries are judged differently than those whose sectors are more robust.

(I) A smart portfolio positioned for long-term growth includes strong stocks from different industries.

As a general rule, it's best to hold stocks from several different industries. That way, if one area of the economy goes into the dumps, you have something to fall back on.

(J) it's smarter to buy and hold good stocks than to engage in rapid-sales trading.

The cost of trading has dropped dramatically. It's easy to find commissions for less than #1.00 a trade. But there are other costs to trading -- including mark-ups by brokers and higher taxes for short-term trades that stack the odds against traders. What's more, active trading requires paying close attention to stock-price fluctuations. That's not so easy to do if you've got a full-time job elsewhere. And it's especially difficult if you are a risk-averse person, in which case the shock of quickly losing a substantial amount of your own money may prove extremely nerve-wracking.

The whole idea is that it is better to hold good stocks with good fundamentals for the long run or do a long term investment on such stocks rather than being a speculator who trades for immediate gains.

2. Mutual Funds
If you have heard the phrase "don't put you egg in one basket", this is simply the whole idea of mutual fund. Mutual found helps to diversify or spread one's investment portfolio.

A mutual fund is a professionally managed investment fund that pools money from many investors to purchase securities such as stocks, shares, real estates and other money market instruments.

Mutual funds are operated by money managers, who invest the fund's capital and attempt to produce capital gains and income for the fund's investors. A mutual fund's portfolio is structured and maintained to match the investment objectives stated in its prospectus.

It gives one an opportunity to enjoy investments in all these securities and help to manage risk or losses. It is less volatile unlike stock because it helps to balance the portfolio. There are many professionally managed mutual fund companies in Nigeria.

One of the main advantages of mutual funds is that they give small investors access to professionally managed, diversified portfolios of equities, bonds and other securities, which would be quite difficult if not impossible to create with a small amount of capital. Each shareholder participates proportionally in the gain or loss of the fund.

3. Treasury Bills & Bond

Treasury Bills are government guaranteed debt instruments issued by the Central bank of Nigeria (CBN). When you buy Treasury bill, you lend to the government. Treasury bills are considered as risk free because they are government guaranteed debt instruments. Usual tenors are 91 days, 182 days and 364 days. Private individuals like you, as well as financial institutions like banks, discount houses, fund managers, can invest in treasury bills.

However, interest received on treasury bills is not subjected to withholding tax and it can be used for collateral for loans and other credit facilities.

Interest on treasury bills is payable upfront giving higher effect yield. While at expiration of the investment the main value can be received or reinvested. Other benefits of investing in Treasury bill are its high liquidity, and the associated risk of loss of value is relatively low.

To invest in treasury bills you can visit you bank. Some banks or discount houses may accept #50,000 and in multiples of #1000 thereafter in your next investment.

A bond on the other hand is a debt security, similar to an I.O.U. When you buy a bond, you are lending money to a government or corporation, federal agency or other entity known as the issuer. In return for the loan, the issuer promises to pay you a specified rate of interest during the life of the bond and to repay the face value of the bond (the principal) when it "matures," or comes due. Bonds enable the issuer to finance long-term investments with external funds.

There are different types of bonds issued for trading by different organizations and governments. Corporate bonds are issued by private and public corporations. Municipal and Government bonds are bonds issued by states, local governments and other government entities. Municipal bonds are exempted from federal, state and local taxes. Foreign bonds are issued by companies outside its country of domiciliation. Asset-backed bonds are bonds backed by pools of assets.

Benefits of investing in bonds include safety and reliability, dependable income, liquidity good yields. Investors in bonds include large financial institutions, such as banks, insurance, managed funds, pension funds, endowments, and mutual funds.

Also Individuals, including low and high-income earners can also invest in bonds.

Maturity date is the date on which the issuer has to repay the nominal amount and how long he can expect to receive interest payments. Maturity period is divided into three categories as follows:

- Short-term with maturities of up to 5 years
- Medium-term with maturities of between 5 and 12 years.
- Long term with maturity of above 12 years.

The three types of interest rates available in bond market are:

Fixed-rate which are payable at regular intervals

Floating rate with interest adjusted periodically according to an index tied to short-term Treasury bills or money markets. Federal Government bonds in Nigeria are adjusted periodically using the Minimum Rediscount Rate (MMR) as the yardstick.

Zero-coupon have no periodic interest payments. They are sold at discount to face value and redeemed at maturity for the full face value. Tax must be paid on the accrued interest every year even though no interest is received

4. Real Estate

The value of land will always appreciate. Have you heard a landlord decrease tenement rate? Have you heard a land owner decrease land price? It simply means this is a profitable business of the future in Nigeria, the fact cannot be denied that the fear of Omo-onile is the beginning of wisdom. The havoc this people have caused is alarming and had made some people to distance from land purchase matters.

However, for me, it's one of the businesses of the 21st century. Land price can appreciate up to 1000% or more if kept for a long period of time as the rate of expansion and development is increasing day by day.

Here are some of the ways you can invest and make your own money in real estate without tears.

(A) Open Space Leasing: This works in a simple and unique way. Buy a property in a good location and lease it out for makeshift use. You can lease it to churches or business that wants to develop a makeshift outlet such as car wash and mechanics. They will be paying you monthly rentage while the property still appreciates for future sell. It is like borrowing money for someone and get paid double interest and still get your money back.

(B) Real Estate Agency: This one is the simplest and easiest of them all. It is not investment per say but service rendering. How it works? Go round and look for properties to let and for sale, advertise your service and help secure clients for the property owners, you will be paid percentage as commission based on the amount the property is sold or rented. You can start with little or no money and if you are smart enough, you will grow to become a giant realtor.

(C) Property Development: This is where the big guys in the industry are doing their stuffs. They acquire properties in nice locations, develop it into luxury apartments, commercial structures, etc and sell at a very high profit margin. They use like N20 million to develop a property and sell for N40 million thereby, making double of their investment.

(D) House/Office Rent – Build a house and put it up for rent, get paid all year for a life time.

(E) Land Flipping: This means buying of land and quickly reselling it for profit. This is one of the smartest investments in the industry and requires no effort whatsoever. Just your money and knowledge and you are good to go. You will need substantial amount if you want to make hundreds of millions but you can start small by buying just one plot and grow to buying tens of plots and acres of lands and keep selling all year round.

CHAPTER 8

THE FINAL DIET

I hope this book as helped in fulfilling its entire idea of enlightening us on what to do in order to live a life of abundance and to meet ever growing financial demands through starting a business and investment.

The practical steps on business expatiated can be adopted and put into practice. In as much as we pray for God's help, we should understand that smart and hard work pays and Heaven only help those who help themselves.

The economic situation of the country is not encouraging though we pray for a better tomorrow but we cannot ascertain when the better tomorrow will come. Every citizen is expected to create his/her own better tomorrow. The better tomorrow of one will ultimately lead to the better tomorrow of all.

This implies that if every individual is financially dependent then the economy of the country will improve because people don't have to wait endlessly seeking what the nation can do for them rather they are seeking what they can do for themselves thereby helping the nation to achieve its general economic goal and development.

It is not a curse, but let be realistic. I encourage paid job because of the experience, entrepreneurial and management exposure that it brings but what if the paid job stops paying today? What if you never get called by any company to pick a job? What if the job you are doing now stops meeting your needs tomorrow? To avoid any of these uncertainties, don't you think you should start trying your hands on any of these tips?

For Business, Sales, marketing and Management consultation.

Contact:

Name: Abimbola Babatunde

Email: tundeabimbola@gmail.com

OR daranifeinvestments@gmail.com

Mobile nos: +2348028481488

+2347033584015

ABOUT THE AUTHOR

Abimbola Tunde holds a National Diploma upper credit in Secretarial Admin of the Osun state Polytechnic Iree, a B.A (Hons) Second Class Upper division in Philosophy of the Olabisi Onabanjo University in 2006, He was an award of service winner during his service years in Kwara state in 2008. He holds a Master of Science in Human resource Management and Industrial relations of the Lagos State University in 2012. He is an Associate Member of the Nigerian Institute of Management (Chartered) and also a Member of the Chartered Institute of Public Management.

He has been a Business Development personnel, management practitioner and a seasoned sales professional in the fund management, IT, ISP and Telecommunication industry from 2008 till date. He is also a business owner and very passionate about doing business.

www.ingramcontent.com/pod-product-compliance
Lightning Source LLC
Chambersburg PA
CBHW081308180526
45170CB00007B/2619